Dopamine detox

Neurotical-science and the
common myths and misconception about
dopamine fasting

Ken N. Anderson

Table of contents

Introduction

CHAPTER 1

- What to know about a dopamine detox
- What is a dopamine detox?
- six compulsive behaviors as targets of the dopamine detox:
- What is dopamine?
- Does a dopamine detox work?
- common myths and misconception about dopamine fasting

Chapter 2
- Mesolimbic pathway to dopamine
- Dopamine theory of addiction
- Theories of addiction definition
- Psychological theories of addiction
- Dopamine and Gaming Addiction

Chapter 3
- Benefits of dopamine detox
- Enhanced Focus
- Mental Well-Being
- Enhanced Creativity

- <u>Clarity Of Thought</u>
- <u>Rediscovery Of Simple Pleasures</u>

<u>Chapter 4</u>
- <u>Staying dedicated to your dopamine detox</u>
- <u>Setting Clear Goals</u>

<u>Chapter 5</u>
- <u>My 6 weeks of dopamine and benefits of dopamine fasting.</u>

<u>Conclusion</u>

Introduction

It's critical to comprehend the complex brain chemistry and the significant impacts of dopamine on our everyday lives. You see, because dopamine generation is so important to motivation and reward, it's commonly referred to as the "pleasure chemical process" in neuroscience. However, it can be somewhat of a sword with two edges in today's environment. You know, addiction and excess stimulation have become rather commonplace. Dopamine fasting is beneficial because of this. Consciously limiting our exposure to stimulants and activities that release dopamine can lead to a host of advantages for our general health. We promise it's worthwhile. We're talking about giving up recreational drugs in order to experience better mental health, more creativity, more solid relationships, and an increased sense of mindfulness. The rewards are truly endless.

In a time where distractions are everywhere and instant gratification is the norm, reducing dopamine levels reminds us of the importance of moderation and taking the time to appreciate life's genuine rewards. It's all about finding that balance.

CHAPTER 1

What to know about a dopamine detox

A dopamine detox, also known as a dopamine fast, entails giving up almost everything that one could find enjoyable, including food, sex, and social interaction.

Proponents claim that by doing this, many contemporary illnesses will be cured, chief among them being poor motivation and lack of attention.

The goal of a dopamine detox is to reduce reward sensitivity by abstaining from dopamine-producing activities, or "pleasures." But the idea of a "dopamine detox" is not supported by studies. The goal of a dopamine detox is to remove oneself from common stimulants like social media, sweets, or going shopping.

Less impulsive lifestyle choices and behaviors take their place. The fasting period may be a few hours or many days long.

It is crucial to understand that a dopamine detox is not a method supported by scientific study.

The majority of the benefits stem from abstaining from potentially addictive activities; evidence of any benefits is anecdotal. They have nothing to do with actually going through a dopamine detox, though.

The entire idea of a "dopamine detox" is based on false science and oversimplifies the functioning of the brain. In actuality, it is significantly more intricate than what this trend of "dopamine detox" implies.

Dopamine detoxes will be covered in more depth in this article, along with any possible hazards and even some unintended ed advantages.

What is a dopamine detox?

To reset your ability to feel dopamine, all you have to do is stop doing anything that makes you happy for a few days. The concept is false, and the name is ridiculous. It's a trend. I'm sure if you stop doing something you enjoy, you'll feel especially fantastic when you resume it—that's not surprising.

Essentially, a dopamine detox is a method of returning your dopamine levels and receptors to normal.

The current spike of dopamine in almost everything we do causes a pleasure/pain imbalance in the brain.

Reading games provides an excellent illustration. Highly exciting. These games provide an excellent experience; otherwise, the industry would not be worth billions of dollars. However, these games have an impact on our rewards system. It all starts off as fun and games, but it eventually leads to an imbalance.

You'll realize that the activity you're doing is no longer as enjoyable; it'll become a need rather than a desire. You lose the sense of delight that came with it at first, and instead you have a sensation of need, despite the fact that the action is not joyful.

This suggests an imbalance. Unfortunately, many people are unaware of how off their levels are. They get numb to it and simply continue with the action.

Because of the indisputable additive nature of gaming, I have done and still do dopamine detoxes. I can tell when I've gone too far with gaming because I monitor my body and mind carefully, contrasting the many emotions as I compare and contrast my baseline and present state of play.

I am there at the moment. I'll probably give myself as many days as I need to reach my baseline or return to my optimal state of mind. They really do work; this is basically a dopamine cleanse.

One excellent method to return to baseline is to undergo a dopamine detox. To be joyful, dopamine release is necessary for all of us, but it must be balanced with our pleasure and pain reward systems.

The fundamental idea behind "detox" is to allow oneself to experience feelings of loneliness or boredom or to try more straightforward activities rather than grabbing for rapid dopamine "hits." In theory, people will begin to recognize the ways in which specific stimuli could divert them.

six compulsive behaviors as targets of the dopamine detox:

- emotional eating
- excessive internet usage and gaming.
- gambling and shopping
- Porn and masturbation
- thrill- and novelty-seeking
- recreational drugs

By fasting from these activities that trigger the brain's neurotransmitters, people become less dependent on the emotional "hits" that dopamine provides, which can sometimes lead to dependence or ad
diction.

What is dopamine?

In the brain, dopamine is one kind of neurotransmitter. It is a chemical messenger that the body naturally produces and affects a variety of behavioral and physiological processes, such as:

- learning
- motivation
- sleep
- mood
- attention

Mental health disorders can be brought on by an excess or shortage of dopamine production. Such diseases, which result in dependency on particular drugs or activities, can be triggered by exposure to excessive levels of stimuli.

Does a dopamine detox work?

A dopamine detox involves avoiding dopamine stimuli for a predetermined amount of time, which can range from one hour to many days.

A person undergoing a dopamine detox must abstain from all forms of excitement, especially those caused by pleasurable stimulants. During the detox, nothing that increases the creation of dopamine is allowed.
Ideally, by the end of the detox, a person will feel more centered, balanced, and less affected by their usual dopamine triggers. However, it is important to note that a true dopamine detox, whereby a person successfully halts all dopamine activity in the brain, is not possible.

Dopamine is produced by the human body on its own, independent of external inputs. A period of abstinence, or "unplugging" from the outside world, would be a more accurate way to characterize the dopamine detox.

Those who occasionally put the technique into practice might benefit from it. But by definition, the term "dopamine detox" is problematic and not at all accurate in terms of science. According to science, the name is not intended to be taken literally.

Does a dopamine detox have benefits?
We have already clarified that a complete and total detox from naturally occurring dopamine is not possible.

Having said that, there may be some health advantages to choosing to disconnect and break free from some impulsive behaviors, like improved focus and mental clarity.

Dopamine is frequently distracting, which could prevent some people from reaching their objectives. It is the reason why some feel-good activities are overdone, and people end up mindlessly scrolling through social media or binge-watching their favorite TV shows.

These pointless obsessions take away from more productively using time for jobs, health objectives, housekeeping, and other things. People may have more time for the things that are more important to them when they intentionally avoid these distractions.To put it briefly, there is no scientific proof that a

dopamine detox is feasible, and any favorable results reported are only anecdotal.
People may be able to get a higher level of mindfulness, though, which has its advantages, by abstaining from some habits, such as spending hours on social media and smart phones. Trusted Source. Reduction of blood pressure, stress, and better sleep are a few of these benefits.

For those struggling with certain addictive behaviors, meditation can be a great way to achieve a state of mindfulness.

The misunderstood version of the "dopamine detox" is little more than a fad, with no scientific evidence to support its effectiveness.

A true "dopamine detox" is impossible because the brain continues to produce dopamine all the time. However, refraining from activities that stem from compulsion and impulse may prove beneficial for short periods of time.

Releasing oneself from mindless TV, fast food, and social media might benefit an individual's
mental health and lifestyle in general, as many of the activities and substances individuals resort to have the potential to become addictive. A "dopamine detox" is not a scientifically validated technique and is, by definition, deceptive; higher mindfulness may be attained by other activities, such as meditation.

common myths and misconception about dopamine fasting

In Western conceptions of the human being, the brain has occupied a dominant position since the end of the nineteenth century. With the development of contemporary experimental techniques for nervous system stimulation and imaging, scientists have amassed irrefutable proof that the brain is the essential physical foundation for human cognition and behavior. Without a doubt, this conclusion has had positive effects on both our medical practice and our self-awareness as a species. But it has also fueled a peculiar form of reductionism: the view that the neural is the primary explanatory level of reality.

This idea is not new; it is neurocentric. A pioneer of neuroanatomy, Nicholas Steno, lamented in 1680 that materialists "do not want to admit... ignorance of the manner in which mind and body unite," viewing the mind as nothing more than a distinct feature of the brain. [2] Many modern conceptions of neuroscience would make Steno cringe in dread. Prominent figures in a range of societal sectors, including education, business, and mental health, now regard the brain as the primary and all-important aspect of human existence. Their service to anthropological reality is harmed by this viewpoint. The neurocentric vision has its costs and commitments, as demonstrated by a recent lifestyle craze in Silicon Valley called

"dopamine fasting." To undertake such a fast, one abstains from all pleasurable stimuli—including food, music, technology, and sexual activity—for a day or longer. Its name reflects the underlying supposition that abstinence from hedonic experiences re-sensitizes us to the action of this neurotransmitter, thereby heightening productivity and
satisfaction following the fast—the way a coffee break helps us become more sensitive to caffeine. Put differently, the goal of dopamine fasting is to temporarily reduce pleasure for therapeutic purposes. Dopamine fasting, which was made popular in 2019 by Dr. Cameron Sepah, a psychiatrist in California, has received some support from the medical community as a possible paradigm for behavior management. Cultural pundits who oppose the degradation of art, communication, and relationships to forms that yield instant gratification also appropriate its conceptual vocabulary. However, the idea is still most well-liked in the IT sector, where people who want to "hack" their biology to perform better at

work are a perfect fit for it. Examining this behavior closely reveals the absurdity of contemporary American Eurocentrism.

system, which causes the release of dopamine, resetting the neurotransmitter receptors in the body. In actuality, dopamine has nothing to do with our pleasure-seeking behavior. Rather, this route facilitates our ability to estimate the expected value of a reward and handle prediction mistakes, which play a far wider role in brain functioning. Stated differently, dopamine is a signal of present unhappiness that drives our motivation and experience-based learning. Furthermore, this holds true for any object we see as valued or judged to be worthwhile, not simply for intrinsically rewarding stimuli like food, sex, and cocaine, due to reciprocal connections with the frontal cortex, the seat of our higher cognitive function. Therefore, dopamine is probably involved in everything that an individual does on a daily basis, including fasting itself.

A real dopamine fast would stop us in our tracks and take away our ability to behave in a goal-directed manner. In fact, mice lacking in any dopaminergic transmission will starve to death and exhibit no desire to eat. Human patients suffering from disorders related to the mesocorticolimbic system frequently exhibit stiffness, delayed movement, difficulty speaking, and a blunting of motivation, concentration, and memory. These may be recognizable to the reader as signs of Parkinson's disease, which is actually brought on by the degeneration of dopamine-producing neurons. To be fair, Sepah has justified his creation by emphasizing that its goal is to lower dopamine levels generated by addictive activities rather than dopamine levels overall. However, in reality, it is utilized and comprehended using the neurobiologically incoherent.

Together with its scientific incoherence, a second and more serious problem with dopamine fasting lies in its underlying philosophical anthropology. The apparently exclusive rooting of this practice in science does not make it ideologically neutral. Instead, it permits it to serve as an effective vehicle for an implicit view of the human person—and, in particular, of the human person's embodied desire.

The first presupposition underlying dopamine fasting is that bodily desire is an optional element of life, an "add-on" that we can (at least temporarily) do without. If experienced at a moderate level, it can be a positive element of our experience. But our default state is one of excessive engagement with the objects of our desire, which enslaves us to cycles of habitual behavior that do not, in fact, align with our higher goals.

One immediately hears a faint echo of the Christian notion of desire, which emphasizes the importance of ordering one's bodily appetites to the good through the virtue of temperance. And insofar as secular "fasting" is predicated upon an intuition of this truth, it will likely bear good fruit. But from here, the implicit philosophy that undergirds this practice takes a turn.

The second presupposition is that the body is a tool for the will. Through the manipulation of brain chemistry, one can intentionally choose and shape the objects of one's desire. By controlling our embodied nature in this way, we can achieve our own self-chosen ends, such as productivity or contentment. For it is personal choice that bestows unity on human experience and meaning upon embodied desire.

This somewhat gnostic yet technocratic understanding of the body is in line with other currents in modern culture, such as the denial of mental illness as anything more than a brain ailment or the control of one's gender identity. It should be noted that this approach to the body does not involve openly disparaging it. Instead, it frequently manifests as a type of sensitivity, an appreciation for the body that, like the inclination toward moderation, underscores the crucial reality that it is deserving of attention. However, there is no mention of the notion that since the body is given, its desires have a natural meaning.

It is helpful to compare this anthropological understanding with the Christian assertion that the body is a sign and sacrament of a divine reality in order to understand what is lost with the lack of givenness. If this is the case, then the way to our fulfillment lies in the nature of the body, including its embodied wants. Without a doubt, we do not follow our nature heedlessly or automatically along this route; rather, we must delve deeply into our experience in order to transition from sign to mystery. We find that "we are not satisfied with what satisfies the body" there, as the Dominican Conrad Pepler puts it, and this discontent prompts us to "search for something higher at the back of all [our] senses can know." The existential search, thus unleashed, does not relent until it seizes upon its true objects: perfect truth, love, justice, and beauty.

But, crucially, the Christian does not leave bodily desire behind in walking this path.

The perfect truth became incarnate. Perfect beauty has the appearance of the face of the fairest of the children of men, Jesus of Nazareth—a man who himself hungered and was satisfied. And the choice of God to enter the horizon of human history and pitch his tent among us continues in the Church, the mystical body of Christ. Thus, the Father draws us to our destiny through physical and emotional, as well as spiritual, attraction to Christ (John 6:44). This method of God redeems the body. Indeed, St. Augustine called the freely extended gift of divine life the "victorious delectation"—in other words, a triumphant desire that wins through every other. Our task is therefore not to flee the body but rather to work, as St. Paul noted, to find and adhere to him by "testing everything and retaining what is good '' (1 Thess 5:21–22).

Because of this, asceticism in the Christian tradition has never been essentially about renunciation but rather about choosing a higher level of fulfillment. It is essentially an affirmation of a more true good than a negative one. Consider the virgin's abstinence from all sexual relations. This most natural manifestation of human affectivity is granted as a good; nonetheless, its temporary renunciation confirms that its significance extends beyond what is immediately perceptible. By practicing chastity, a Christian might come to know his spouse on a deeper level: a love that views her as a mystery, not an object, a sign from the Mystery Himself, the only one who can genuinely satisfy each person's heart. More dramatically still, individuals who are called to this renunciation as a stable state of life discover through the path of virginity a nuptial relationship with that very mystery, thereby anticipating and witnessing to the eternal wedding banquet that awaits all who draw to themselves. The acetic word of loving chastely is humanly fulfilling; it makes us whole.

So, acknowledging the body's inherent give-and-take opens up new possibilities for fasting and, in fact, for any kind of renunciation. As secular fasting aims to do, it does more than just help us develop self-control and resensitize us to things we take for granted. Instead, it speaks of a more profound ownership of the same things we refrain from. Because the feast is when a sincere fast finds its purpose. Thus, when a Christian grows in virtue, her bodily delight increases; after all, she is "still full of sap and still green" (Psalm 92:14), even in her old age. Who wouldn't want such a life?

This other understanding of desire is not only stronger, but it also makes more sense in light of current scientific findings about the brain. Because, as the aforementioned research highlights, human behavior is driven by want, and a person cannot exist without it. Although natural cues initially move our embodied motivation, they do not satisfy it and, if regarded as its primary or exclusive goal, can even lead to enslavement. However, we cannot arbitrarily replace the objects of our desire by severing our physical pleasures, as the secular fast suggests. Rather, the natural orientation of our brain structure is to integrate our innate desires

with our higher-order judgments and beliefs in a continual pursuit of something. Therefore, maybe there's no need for our civilization to instantly abandon its neurocentric viewpoint. Alternatively, maybe excessive interest in the brain can be a means of retrieving what is in danger of being lost. For example, delving further into brain research on dopamine fasting exposes a prophecy regarding the meaning of embodied desire: attraction to
our destiny. According to

Studies i: *One phenomenon above all underlies the vibrant arc of human life . . . it is the common essence of every human interest, the driver of every problem: it is the phenomenon of desire . . . Desire, which is the expression of our human life, ultimately incarnates the profound attraction with which God calls us to Himself.*

I did a dopamine fast - here's why it was amazing for my productivity

Dopamine fasting has nothing to do with changing the dopamine levels in your brain. Instead, fasting gives you the time and space to reflect on the root causes of your behavior. Don't approach a fast without thinking about mapping out and reflecting on your behaviors.

I recently took part in a dopamine fast because of the hype. I abstained from all activities for the entire day, with the exception of strolling, thinking, and writing. It was really helpful, and I felt especially concentrated in the days that followed. But there are a lot of misconceptions about dopamine fasting. I wish to debunk these misconceptions based on my personal study and practice so that you can approach dopamine quickly and appropriately. In this

post, I want to explain what dopamine
fasting is, isn't, and what you should
genuinely hope to learn from it. I'll explain
how I went about the fast, why it wasn't a
good idea, and what you may take away from
it in the next sections of this important point
of a dopamine fast despite its lack of effect
on dopamine.

Before I dive into this, I want to make it clear
that I'm not a doctor, medical practitioner, or
behavioral psychology expert. This said, the
sources I cite throughout the article are
written by experts. I'm aiming to sift through
a lot of the noise that exists on the topic of
dopamine fasting and provide you with the
right mindset and tools to approach fasting
that are backed up by these experts.

The science

I'm going to start off pretty blunt. Dopamine
fasting has very little to do with lowering
dopamine levels in your brain. The term
"dopamine fast" is nothing more than a sexy

marketing name that differentiates it from its true nature. In essence, dopamine fasting is a cognitive behavioral therapy technique. If you approach this with the expectation that you're changing the neurochemical reactions in your brain, you're going to have a rough time. I'll tell you why.

Reintroducing a dopamine-generating activity does not result in increased levels of dopamine in the brain after the deprivation period, according to a study on the effects of dopamine levels in rats after self-administered dopamine binges and a 1 or 7-day period of deprivation. In other words, stopping an activity won't cause your dopamine to reset. This is significant since a lot of people appear to think that fasting can change the tolerance levels in the dopamine system.

What, then, is the purpose of dopamine fasting if it isn't to raise dopamine levels? Phenotypic fasting is a type of cognitive behavioral therapy, as I briefly explained in this section's introduction (CBT). Cognitive-behavioral therapy (CBT) redefines your connection to your behavior. It is usually used in an organized approach during therapy conversations to address harmful or ineffective behaviors that stem from people's beliefs about their own actions. CBT urges you to utilize the model of classical conditioning to investigate the causes of your behavior.

Since the classical conditioning model provides the framework for behavior modification, it is crucial to the dopamine fasting process. According to the theory of classical conditioning, we behave in certain ways because of environmental cues that, when we respond to them, provide us with rewards. We are motivated to repeat the behavior by this incentive. We can redefine our relationship with our conduct through dopamine fasting. You can experience what happens when you don't act on impulse by choosing not to perform the action you would normally do (like browsing Instagram while you're bored at work). It is this process's outcome that will alter your beliefs.

vior.

- Dopamine fasting doesn't starve your brain of dopamine

- There is no reset button on the neurochemical processes that occur in your brain

- The goal of dopamine fasting is to give you space and time to reflect on what your behaviors do for you

- Aim to redefine your relationship with your behavior

Does Dopamine Detox/Fasting work or is it just a fad?

Let's get things straight about dopamine detox. Is it an elegant solution to unwanted behaviors and increased happiness, or just a maladaptive fad? Some people are saying it helped them feel better, so should you try it as well? Does it work?

Dopamine and Dopamine Fasting

You might assume it must be effective if the dopamine detox YouTube videos have received scores of millions of views. That strategy has a flaw in it since the people who made these dopamine detox films have a very narrow knowledge of the functions that dopamine plays in our brains. No, dopamine is not limited to motivation and rewards. It is a sophisticated neuromodulator that plays a key role in many vital processes, including movement, attention, learning, memory, mood, time perception, sleep, and even delayed reward. Furthermore, most individuals are unaware that dopamine is constantly released through a process known as "tonic" dopamine release, in addition to the "phasic" releases that are linked to pleasurable stimuli. Dopamine is therefore required for multiple important functions, and it is always present in your brain. Dopamine detox implies that dopamine is a toxin, which, as you know, is absorbed. But even using 'dopamine fasting' is just plain wrong. If you could fast or deprive your brain of dopamine, it would be truly tragic for you. There are people with brain damage who have low levels of dopamine. What is their life like? They struggle to move, swallow, or even talk, and they often suffer from depression and other emotional changes. Of course, they have heard of this condition, which is called Parkinson's disease. Another way to effectively lower dopamine levels is by using powerful pharmaceuticals that block dopamine receptors in the brain. Dr. Andrew Huberman reported how he felt after he was given a dopamine antagonist (receptor blocker). He was crying and felt more depressed, hopeless, and miserable than ever in his entire life. In summary, fasting from dopamine in your brain would be your worst nightmare. And, of course, you won't even get there without powerful drugs or brain damage.

Dopamine Fasting Effectiveness

Alright, so those who support dopamine might not really know everything there is to know about it. They might, nevertheless, still be endorsing a beneficial and useful product. Let's be kind and assume that, in spite of what they say, what they really want is for you to avoid doing anything that raises your dopamine release levels—not to detox or fast from dopamine. Regretfully, when we consider what should be avoided during a dopamine detox, we find that things like junk food, music, computers, phones, and the internet release as much or even less dopamine as natural activities like having sex, working out, being in the cold, or even socializing with others. This implies that the activities you will abstain from will only be those that cause a significant dopamine release. However, that's not all. Even if that argument were invalid, if you could eliminate for one whole day (as the protocol states) all high dopamine-releasing activities to try to upregulate your dopamine receptors, it would still not work. For a meaningful and lasting change, you will need weeks, not a single day. Abstaining for at least 30 continuous days. So really, following all these popular dopamine detox protocols will do very little for you.

Twisted Concept

But putting all the popular internet dopamine detox gurus aside, the concept was originally popularized by psychologist Dr. Cameron Sepah. He admits that most people promoting dopamine detox have twisted his argument. Contrary to the name dopamine detox or fasting, the goal is not to reduce dopamine but to reduce the "time spent on problematic behaviors.".

So there you have it: dopamine detox or fasting is not about detoxing, is not about fasting, and is not even about dopamine. It is about problematic behaviors. It is quite shocking that a person who popularized the concept decided to use a name that has little to do with the actual intervention. And given that terrible name, you really cannot blame wellness gurus and YouTubers for how they twisted the concept. And no wonder that people who know their stuff call dopamine detox a maladaptive fad, or pseudoscience.

Band-aid Results

Now that we are aware that problematic activities, rather than dopamine, are the cause of the detox, we may deduce that "dopamine detox" really refers to abstaining from harmful behaviors. Let me clarify: isn't that what our grandmothers have been telling us for thousands of years? "Avoid negative actions." What a waste of a chic new trend! Naturally, you will feel better for a while if you cut out unpleasant or problematic behaviors and increase the frequency of positive ones (such as journaling, reading, meditating, and going outside). This clarifies why some who have experienced "dopamine detox" claim that it temporarily improved their mood. However, the issue with "dopamine detox" is that it ignores the underlying causes of people's troublesome behaviors in the first place. Because of that, people gradually return to their bad habits after their detox, meaning it doesn't work; it's only a band-aid.

What to do instead

So, if you really want to change and improve, forget about dopamine detox. Instead, learn how to manage and leverage your dopamine system. If you do, some of your problems will immediately cease to be problems, while others could be eradicated and replaced with something better.

Chapter 2

Mesolimbic pathway to dopamine

classified as obesity-prone show low basal DA levels in the NAc prior to obesity onset, suggesting that alterations in the dopaminergic system may precede changes in behavior. Clinical research has also provided evidence for altered dopaminergic processes associated with binge eating; among binge-eating individuals, increased DA levels in the striatum are associated with the severity of binge eating.

Dopamine theory of addiction

The idea that addiction is a dopamine neurotransmitter system issue has been around for a number of decades, but it hasn't produced any novel treatments. In this opinion piece, we go over the history of the dopamine theory of addiction and talk about how addictive substances might cause the striatum to release dopamine. While there is strong evidence that stimulants raise striatal dopamine levels and some evidence that alcohol may also have this effect, there is little to no evidence that opiates and cannabis do the same. Furthermore, there is strong evidence that people with stimulant or alcohol dependence have decreased striatal dopamine receptor availability and dopamine release, but not people with opiate, nicotine, or cannabis dependence. These findings have consequences. For understanding reward and treatment responses in various addictions.

When participating in addictive activity, addicts experience a lack of control and an inability to stop. People develop tolerance with time, and when they stop receiving the same level of satisfaction from the thing they are hooked on, their addictive behavior increases. Over time, addiction can take over a person's life to the point where they stop

caring for their obligations and engaging in other activities. Addiction is still a major issue that negatively impacts the mental and physical well-being of many people, as well as the communities in which they live. For the purpose of developing effective preventive and treatment plans, psychologists should have a solid understanding of addiction.
s.

Theories of addiction definition

Let's start by defining what we mean by addiction. Although we often associate addiction with illegal drugs, it can also apply to many other things like alcohol, cigarettes, prescription medication or even rewarding behaviors like gambling, gaming or using the internet.

Theories of addiction: Understanding addiction

Theories of addiction attempt to explain addiction in terms of general principles (e.g., genetic inheritance or operant conditioning). Both biological and psychological theories of addiction have been proposed, with the former highlighting the influence of nature and the latter the influence of nurture on addiction.

Psychological theories of addiction

The learning hypothesis, a psychological theory of addiction, focuses on how nurture—or our upbringing—shapes our behavior. The learning theory delineates multiple mechanisms by which an individual's environment shapes their addictive behavior.

Classical conditioning

Through the process of classical conditioning, we can learn to associate an unconditional stimulus (like food) with a neutral stimulus that triggers an instinctive biological response. Because of this, we naturally react conditionally—for example, by salivating—to the neutral stimulus. The way classical conditioning operates is by linking environmental signals to reflexive actions. We need only think back to the well-known Pavlov experiment, in which he trained dogs to salivate in response to the ringing of a bell, to understand how classical conditioning operates. According to the theory of classical conditioning, environmental signals connected to addictive behaviors might serve as triggers, creating a strong desire to engage in the habit.

Operant conditioning

Operant conditioning is a learning method in which actions are reinforced with rewards and deterred with punishment.
Behaviors that result in a positive outcome will be repeated, but behaviors that result in a bad end will be discontinued, according to the theory of operant conditioning.

Both behavioral and substance addictions are associated with the reward system of the brain. Every time we engage in the behavior, our brain is flooded with dopamine, which acts as a positive reinforcer.

Addiction can also be strengthened because people use it to avoid problems and cope with physical pain or negative emotions. In these situations, the absence of pain is a negative reinforcer.

Over time, drug addicts frequently learn to use their addiction not for the rush of the high but rather to fend off the unpleasant physical and psychological symptoms of syndrome. Positive punishments, like withdrawal symptoms, reduce a person's likelihood of trying to stop in the future.

Losing confidence, euphoric feelings, or friends may also be part of the process of beating an addiction. These are illustrations of Over time, drug addicts frequently learn to use their addiction not for the rush of the high but rather to fend off the unpleasant physical and psychological symptoms of withdrawal syndrome. Positive punishments, like withdrawal symptoms, reduce a person's likelihood of trying to stop in the future.
. The process of quitting your addiction might also involve losing friends, feelings of euphoria, or one's confidence. These
are
examples of negative punishment which discourage people from quitting.

What is the Dopamine Theory of Addiction

The dopamine theory of addiction is the staple of modern psychology for treating addictions, including reading game addiction.

It's important to understand how our brains respond to the stimulus of reading games. A lot of research is needed to fully understand how the mechanism of a dopamine release experienced when playing reading games is similar to the dopamine release experienced with drugs and other addictive substances. The theory of dopamine addiction may offer insight into how the regulation and release of dopamine are crucial for treating and understanding why gamers develop gaming problems.

Dopamine detox

In brief, the hypothesis contends that decreased dopamine function in addicted subjects results in a decreased interest in non-drug-related stimuli and increased sensitivity to the drug of choice, leading to the proposition that restoring dopamine function might be therapeutically advantageous."

An addiction causes our bodies to produce so much more dopamine when the drug or stimulus is removed that our bodies are unable to produce the same quantity of dopamine on their own. Thus, the only thing that can increase dopamine to the necessary levels in an addicted person is the substance or the stimuli to which they are dependent.

Hence, the secret to beating an addiction is to get the body to produce dopamine again naturally, independent of drugs or the trigger that is causing the addiction.

"**What is Dopamine?**
Dopamine is a neurotransmitter in our brains responsible for the feeling of pleasure. Our body produces it when we feel pleasure, and it is then transmitted to nerve cells.

Numerous physiological processes are impacted by dopamine, including learning, motivation, blood vessels, heart rate, kidneys, sleep, mood, breastfeeding, movement, attention, and nausea. An individual's inherent capacity to create dopamine is disrupted when they are hooked. The only time their dopamine production is enough is when they take the drug, drink another glass of alcohol, or play another round of their favorite reading game. Since the mid–1950s, scientists have learned that addictions are caused by the disruption of dopamine production in the affected person's brain.

In 1954, some students conducted a study on rats to determine where dopamine is produced in the brain.

Rats were first placed in a large-levered Skinner box to begin the experiment. The rats could press the lever in this box because of the way it was configured. The rats would get electrical stimulation to the septic region of the brain, also referred to as the pleasure center, when the lever was pulled.

The experiment included "acquisition" and "extinction" periods. The acquisition was when rats pressed the button, and they received electrical shocks. The extinction period was when the electrical current was blocked, even if the rats pressed
he lever.

The results?

When rats got an electrical pulse into their pleasure centers during the acquisition period, the vast majority of lever presses occurred. Nevertheless, the rats ceased to press the lever upon cutting the current. The lack of a reward made them lose motivation to pull the lever.

The rats experienced pleasure when they pressed the lever, so they kept pressing it.

What made the rats press the lever to get the electric current, even if it was stronger, was that it was hitting their reward centers in their brains. It's the same center responsible

for making us feel happy when we eat or
have sex.

This experiment was the first major
milestone that today helps us learn how
addictions work through dopamine.

Some of the more important studies and
experiments were done after 1954.
include:

- A positive reinforcement study from
  the 1970s found that drugs provide
  positive reinforcement for dopamine
  release, which confirmed that
  stimulants such as drugs could increase
  dopamine creation.
- Researchers also found that blocking
  dopamine receptors decreases the
  effects of some drugs.
- Another important discovery came
  from Sardinia, where researchers found
  that addictive drugs release dopamine
  while non-addictive drugs do not.

Dopamine is crucial for the creation of addictive habits.

It has long been thought that the dopamine released after drug use causes the euphoria we feel right after using the drug.

It has long been believed that dopamine release when taking drugs directly releases the euphoria that we experience shortly after taking drugs.

However, more recent studies show that dopamine is likely a reinforcing agent for taking more of the drug. It makes an addicted person crave the drug more. Once we go through a pleasant experience, dopamine is released.

We feel extreme exhilaration shortly after using drugs, and our brains' reward systems become active. Additionally, dopamine begins to be released at that point, which results in brain alterations that facilitate drug reuptake. Sadly, this leads to difficult-to-break compulsive patterns.

It gets harder and harder for someone who is hooked on drugs to feel pleasure. They no longer generate the required levels of dopamine from natural activities that do so, including sex or a balanced diet, which makes them feel flat. Rather, the addict can only be satisfied by higher dosages of drugs, which can eventually result in an overdose.

Now, you might be thinking: Why are you talking about drug addictions when this site is about gaming addiction?

The answer is that many drug addictions act similar to gaming addictions in terms of dopamine production. Thus, the dopamine theory of addiction is also applicable to reading game addiction, which we'll talk about in a bit more detail.

later on.

Overcoming Drug Addiction

It is more difficult to overcome a drug addiction (or any other addiction, for that matter, including a gaming addiction) because addictions alter the way our brains function.

Abruptly stopping medications causes the body to stop producing the same amounts of dopamine naturally. Severe drug withdrawal symptoms could result from this, including:

- Depression
- Anxiety
- Bad mood
- Muscle cramps and spasms
- Constipation
- Fatigue, low energy
- Low energy
- And several others

Numerous symptoms of low dopamine levels are comparable to these ones. When an addict stops using a substance for a few days, their body can no longer manufacture dopamine at the same rate, which causes withdrawal symptoms. Additionally, the body is physically adapting to life without these medicines. We'll need to follow a stringent drug detox in order to undo these modifications in our levels of dopamine production. This may take a few weeks or months, and only if the detox was sufficiently intense would the effects become apparent.

Dopamine and Gaming Addiction

"When we play reading games, our brains release large amounts of dopamine. These levels are similar to the dopamine levels when we take drugs like amphetamine or methylphenidate."

Playing games floods our brains' reward circuitry with dopamine. Naturally, when we play reading games, we only get a brief spike in dopamine, but it's enough to give us a sense of joy and excitement. These dopamine spikes that occur following a game may be similar to the release of dopamine during drug use.

The rush you get when you want to kill the next boss in the game or face an enemy is similar to when taking drugs. Your heart rate will increase, and your focus will stay solely on the game; everything else becomes unimportant at that moment. This can be a flow state.

Sound familiar?

An addiction to gaming will cause the brain to become accustomed to the extra-cheap dopamine that comes from reading games. Therefore, when we don't play reading games, it won't make dopamine on its own. This can result in a variety of mental health issues, much like drug and alcohol abusers do.

Some of the most common mental health problems that gaming addicts experience when they don't get their dose of games.

Chapter 3

Benefits of dopamine detox

The benefits of a dopamine detox are pretty amazing and can have a positive impact on different areas of your life. Check it out:

Weight Management

You may find it easier to properly control your weight and develop healthier eating habits if you limit the amount of food that causes dopamine to be released and refrain from overindulging.

This newfound awareness and control can empower you to make more conscious choices when it comes to your diet, leading to long-lasting positive changes in your overall health and well-being.

Enhanced Focus

Engaging in a dopamine detox, a practice designed to reduce distractions and enhance concentration, can have a profound impact on your ability to stay focused on tasks and accomplish more.

Consciously reducing your exposure to dopamine-releasing media, like video games and social media, makes room for more productivity and mental clarity. Accepting this cleansing might result in increased awareness and a better feeling of general well-being.

Digestive Health

When you make a conscious effort to steer clear of processed and sugary foods during a detox, you can significantly contribute to improving your digestive health.

By removing these kinds of items from your diet, you lower your chance of developing common problems like bloating and indigestion. This change in diet enables your body to concentrate on more effectively absorbing vital nutrients, supporting general health and a more wholesome digestive system.

Mental Well-Being

Resetting your brain's reward system during a detox involves breaking free from addictive behaviors and habits, allowing for a fresh start, and paving the way for improved mental well-being.

You can lessen your symptoms of anxiety and depression by avoiding drugs and behaviors that overstimulate the reward system, such as binge-watching social media or overindulging in unhealthy meals.

This process enables you to recalibrate your brain, fostering a healthier mindset and enhancing overall emotional resilience.

Natural Reward Appreciation

By stepping away from artificial stimulants like incessant messages and screen time, you can detach and appreciate the wonders of the natural world.

By stepping away from the digital realm, you open yourself up to a whole new level of appreciation and enjoyment for the simple pleasures and natural rewards that surround you.

Accepting these sensations can create a sense of contentment and serenity that transcends artificial stimulation, whether it's the sound of birds chirping, the scent of fresh flowers, or the feel of soft grass beneath your feet. Thus, give yourself a moment to detach, relax, and allow the wonders of nature to fascinate your senses.

Improved Sleep Patterns

By consciously reducing the amount of time spent on dopamine-inducing screens and activities such as social media and video games, you might start to observe a remarkable improvement in the quality and patterns of your sleep.

This occurs because prolonged exposure to these stimulants might throw off your body's natural circadian rhythm and make it more difficult for you to wind down and rest. Thus, by deliberately trying to reduce your exposure, you allow your body and mind to re-calibrate and reap the healing effects of a restful night's sleep.

Enhanced Creativity

Engaging in detoxes can create valuable mental space for your creativity to flourish since you won't be constantly hacking into your brain's reward pathways.

Detoxes free your mind to concentrate on discovering new concepts and broadening your creative boundaries by getting rid of distractions and decreasing the constant need for dopamine surges.

Your creative endeavors may benefit from a greater degree of creativity and inventiveness thanks to your newly discovered clarity and liberation from addictive impulses. Thus, seize the chance to cleanse your system, allow your brain to naturally manufacture dopamine, and unleash the entire creative potential within.
you!

Strengthened Relationships

Reducing the amount of time spent on screens allows for more opportunities to engage in meaningful interactions with loved ones.

You can make time for meaningful interactions, shared experiences, and treasured moments that can fortify and enhance your relationships by putting down your electronic gadgets. Accepting this deliberate decision might help you feel more fulfilled, connected, and understood in your relationships with others.

Increased Patience And Tolerance

Detoxing can be a transformative process that not only helps you become more patient and tolerant of delays and inconveniences but also allows you to shift your focus away from immediate rewards.

It is possible to develop a mindset that accepts delayed gratification and values the trip just as much as the goal by deliberately placing a higher value on long-term advantages and personal development. So start your detoxification adventure and see how it might improve your general health and attitude toward life.

Heightened Awareness And Mindfulness

Taking the time to disconnect from excessive stimulation, such as the constant barrage of notifications and distractions, can truly cultivate a greater sense of mindfulness and self-awareness.

Through purposeful facilitation of calm meditation and self-awareness of our thoughts and feelings, we enable ourselves to gain a deeper comprehension of both the self and the external environment. Taking a deliberate break from the chaos might increase one's sense of inner serenity and clarity.

Reconnection With Nature

Detoxes often encourage spending more time outdoors, immersing oneself in the beauty of nature, and fostering a deeper connection with the natural world.

Enjoying the outdoors can make your detox process seem more serene and rejuvenating, whether it's through leisurely strolls in the park, taking in the clean air, or just taking in the brilliant colors of the surroundings.

Clarity Of Thought

Starting a systematic detoxification program can have a significant impact on your ability to think clearly and make decisions since you will be dependent only on dopamine, which occurs naturally.
If you free yourself from the constant craving for instant gratification, you create space for more deliberate and thoughtful choices, ultimately leading to a greater sense of overall well-being.

.

Rediscovery Of Simple Pleasures

When we intentionally cleanse our bodies and brains during a detox, we frequently find a renewed sense of delight in the small, everyday joys that are sometimes overlooked in the midst of the craziness of our hectic, overstimulating lives. You'll discover how to recognize and manage dopamine triggers, ensuring that any dopamine released is entirely organic.

From savoring the warmth of a freshly brewed cup of herbal tea to relishing the gentle touch of a cool breeze against our skin, these small moments of bliss become cherished reminders of the beauty and tranquility that surround us.

In general, a dopamine detox is a means of regaining equilibrium in a world full of pursuits and materials that continually arouse the reward centers of our brains. It might lessen the negative effects of excessive dopamine-inducing behaviors and help you appreciate life's small pleasures, which can lead to a healthier and more fulfilled life.
ing.

Chapter 4

Staying dedicated to your dopamine detox

Setting Clear Goals

Setting specific objectives is crucial for the dopamine detoxification process. Setting attainable goals gives the detox process focus and dedication, whether it be a full stop to stimulating activities for a predetermined number of days or a progressive reduction in exposure.

Creating a Detox Schedule

The secret to successful implementation is creating a comprehensive timetable that specifies the detox period and substitute, non-stimulating activities. This could entail setting out particular periods of time for concentrated work, physical activity, hobbies, and social connections that don't rely on artificial or digital stimuli.

Engaging in Non-Stimulating Activities
During the detox period, individuals are encouraged to engage in activities that do not elicit a significant dopamine response. These activities may include reading, outdoor walks, meditation, creative pursuits, and other forms of mindful engagement.

Reflecting and Assessing Progress
A crucial component of the detoxification process is regular introspection and self-evaluation. People ought to keep a journal of their experiences, including any difficulties, successes, or changes in their concentration and productivity. This contemplative exercise acts as a motivating tool and helps to comprehend the effects of dopamine detox.

Chapter 5

My 6 weeks of dopamine and benefits of dopamine fasting.

I'm six weeks into my dopamine detox, andI'm feeling good. First off, I wanted this to be a long-term lifestyle change and not just a 24-hour challenge.

So this is not exactly a detox but more like a sustainable dopamine reduction—in other words, reducing instant gratification as a lifestyle change—something that I might be able to do for the rest of my life. In my opinion, the idea of that24-hour detox is just like bait for some people.
 We're advising you to do nothing that gives you dopamine: not listen to music, not read, not exercise. In my opinion, that's just

stupid. This is for self-improvement. We want to be better than we are right now. We want to make progress, and that comes from not just a 24-hour challenge but from setting a kind of lifestyle that we can stick to for a very long time.

So aroundMay 12th is when I started implementing this, and that was about six weeks ago. I'll have my behavior tracker to see whether or not you believe this because honestly, whatI'm showing you is real, but what was I like before I started the detox?

pretty much the hardest that ever worked was just above the bare minimum. I graduated from university with literally the bare minimum grade. For most of my adult life, I Haven't done any kind of extra work other than go to the gym, which is the one thing I've kind of stayed consistent with.

 It's just lifting weights, so after college and after university, honestly, I'd skipped most of those days anyway, but after those days, I'd come home, lift weights, and thenI'd play

Runescape. I scroll on Redditand Instagram
so damn much. I like Instagram memes,
scrolling on the front page, and just seeing
all the little articles and feeling like you've
learned something.

It was just howI spend all my time, and I was
definitely spending at least 6 hours a day on
social media, in particular Instagram. I was
obsessed with SnapChat.

I was always obsessed. I was posting to these,
like, you know, annual snapshot stories. I
was the guy who had like a thirty- to forty-
second Snapchat story every single day. I just
felt the need to show everyone what I was
doing. I thought everyone was interested to
see like four pictures of me in just different
flex poses in these six weeks. Honestly, they
have gone so slowly, which is so weird to say
because obviously.
What you know is that when you become an
adult, you start saying that the time goes
really fast when you're not wasting your time
on easy dopamine's on these instant
gratification activities; the time just goes so

slow when you reduce instant gratification.
You simply have more time and brainpower
left in the day, like for you to just expend.

I realize that there are two pathways that you
can go into and you do this. The first one, in
my opinion, is definitely the wrong way to do
it. This is where you reduce the dopamine,
you reduce the instant gratification, but then
you haven't added anything else to your
schedule, so after you've reduced it and
you've got all this free time, you end up just
wasting time, you end up just lying around,
and after your 24-hour challenges
or you just go back to scrolling on your
phone; that's the wrong way to do it.

We're doing this because we want self-
improvement.
You want to make better progress than you
did yesterday, so that is the wrong way to do
it. A better way, in my opinion, is to reduce
those dopamine's, reduce that instant
gratification, and then, with all of that time,
energy, and brain power that you have that
you haven't used for social media and all that

[___]] then you need to increase your delayed gratification. gratification You must know and schedule the activities that are like hard work but give you a reward if you just reduced the instant dopamine's you haven't done much.

People say that you're cured of fried receptors, and maybe you will, and maybe you'll feel a bit better and your mental health will get better if you're not using social media, but you won't really achieve anything more than rehabilitation like recovery, and while that's good with all the new free time you've got, you should obviously be investing it into it.

Something that I actually am going gonna give you a major benefit in the future is an action I can take like an hour a day, and it gives me some rewards in the long term, so there were few that I found that I've made plenty of videos on, and it seems like it's helping other people.
As well which is mindfulness so that's built through "meditation gratitude that is

improved through gratitude journaling and writing letters of gratitude"

 they were my two new habits that I added and you can see from my behavior tracker that I've been so consistent with these from May 12th I've missed two days of gratitude journaling I haven't even missed a single day of meditation I've taken two days off exercising honestly from May 12 I've only taken two days as rest days only because my knees were clicking a lot.

 I'm so proud of myself for this change now I won't lie that I already had you know the years of exercise of lifting experience beforehand so I already felt like I was chat like I was muscular beforehand so the picture that I'll probably have for my thumbnail it's not just like I you know I made this muscle in six weeks what I did make in six weeks though changes that I didn't really expect to make.
I have always been a binge eater. I eat like I eat so much junk food, and I Was proud to say that because I was still making muscle at

the same time, and come on, who doesn't want to be able to eat all the nice foods that they want and also actually build a decent physique at the same time? I always knew that that wasn't the optimum, that wasn't like the 100% effort if possible. The best-case scenario was to be lifting as heavy as and consistent as possible.

Iwas but also to get my diet checked, and in five to six years of training, Inever fixed up my diets. Suddenly, I did this dopamine detox, and in the last month, my diet has been flawless. I went back to tracking calories and

I've Actually been eating clean. I've actually been structuring cheat days, and like, my cheat days are what my normal days used to be. I'm in the best shape of my life. I've lost like 4 pounds in the last month, just from June 1st to June 30th, before I started this dopamine detox.

What I found really weird was thatI wasn't even enjoying the instant gratification of the easy dopamine acts that I was doing. I just had a conversation with my friend yesterday about this, where you'd be watching movies or playing games but your mind wouldn't switch off. You were still thinking and planning and just wanting to achieve more and more because we've got that self-improvement mindset.

Self-improvement is obviously a good thing. You're making even more progress than everyone else. Obviously, now whitmore meditation experience, I realized that this is just not being mindful. We're not mindful when we're playing games or watching movies. Some people are, and maybe respect them because if you can just sit down and shoot out the world and involve yourself in a movie, a game, or something like that,.

Honestly, it must be nice, but personally, I can't if I sit down and stick a movie on like I just can't concentrate. I'm like looking at the movie for like business ideas I'm looking at.the movie for like inspiration and motivation I'm not looking at the movie in

terms of what the movie actually is; I'm just
thinking and planning because I don't want
to waste that time, and you know some
people will say it's not a waste. Because
You're enjoying it, but obviously if I'm not
enjoying it, it is a waste of time, and I lived
like that for so long that Ispent like an entire
year where this was just my normal day-to-
day experience.

 Whereas whatever fun activity I was doing, I
wasn't even having fun. You know, obviously
that's a major symptom of depression, and I
thought I was fully depressed, and maybe it
is depression, but honestly, what I've
realized is that it's it or it's only really
depression, and it's only really negative if
you don't listen to your brain, like your brain
is literally telling you what it is.

It would rather be my fault, like the weak
version of me, than his fault, like my fault
for sitting down and watching a movie when
clearly my brain wanted to, like, think of
stuff and he wanted to do other things but all
of that time I should have just listened to my

brain because it literally wanted me to go and do hard work for a really long time it felt like I wanted to do like a dopamine detox without even knowing what it was.

 if I'm not if you're not enjoying anything that you're currently doing other than the hard work so I was obviously enjoying going through the gym I was enjoying that's the only productive thing I was doing honestly and I was like like going to work I was working part-time at the time and I actually used to enjoy going to work because I'd take my laptop on a night shift and then do more business work on the shift.

So I enjoyed that stuff more than I enjoyed being sat watching TV. I enjoy the healthy meals that fit my macronutrients more than those binge meals because those are just that kind of instant gratification. It is honestly a weakness. It's like these companies.

Businesses have found a way to just spike that part of us that makes us desire those things but,

I don't think we truly want that though
because you just you don't feel happy whilst
you're doing it you don't feel happy
afterwards but look at me when I'm in the
gym I'm smiling I'm literally dancing around
and singing and rapping and beatboxing and
stuff and I'm like in such a happy fun mood
when I'm in the gym and then look at me
when I'm watching a movie and I'll literally
just be sat there like
I've literally just sat there like this and you
just mouth breathe while you watch.

 The point is you're obviously not even
enjoying it and you laugh once or twice over
the entire one-and-a-half hour movie. What
is the point? It is literally just a time wasting
activity where you could have gone and made
some gains, you could have gone and made
some money during that time you could have
gone and developed your business.

Your mentality your ma your mindfulness
your mental health instead you're just doing
what you think is like normal because

Everyone else does it. I hated living like that. I couldn't live like that. I can't believe I spent so much time with that. It's just my normal life because I just kind of didn't. It didn't all click. Hopefully this if you haven't already made this change.

Hopefully with aid go you know it just clicks and it just makes sense now let's talk about some downsides because there is some downsides to this in fact come on bro ah hey pop my head with the phone well if you talk about some downsides I'm just gonna go hit some tricep dips my elbows were clicking as I did this before so I'm getting some joint pain recently.
So I've been taking some extra time to do some rehab recovery work. My elbow clicked on those exercises as well. If you know how to stop that elbow pain let me know so there are some downsides to this dopamine detox lifestyle.

No one else seems to mention them because obviously I've got like a negative view of youtubers because I feel like they just sell you

like the basic idea and then don't really tell
you the real experience because obviously
they're busy and they've only done this
dopamine detox for like one day whereas you
know the real person who's done it for six six
weeks.
 or something will tell you that there is
downsides to this so the first downside is
loneliness it's losing what you considered
was friends when you use social media you
really do feel connected to everyone now I've
got like a thousand followers or just under a
thousand followers on social media and I
follow like I'm a bit of.

 I only follow like a hundred of them back so
when you scroll on social media it does make
your brain feel nice it makes you feel like you
just connected to these people you see
pictures off so when you see something about
someone posting their achievement they've
just graduated from uni or you see like them
post in a your that'd be is massive you know
the reading doesn't even do it justice that's
how the biggest B I've seen those dark eyes
I'm gonna leave you alone if you don't come

towards me otherwise that wasp flew into my room yesterday and I grabbed a towel so that wicking towel action.
 That you do and just hit the wasp with it straight away and they started lying all over the place when I lost it for like ten minutes and I got really scared because it was in my room somewhere I didn't know where to find out what's weird about me.

Describing this right now these things are so much more fun and enjoyable now like just literally seeing a Big B was like the highlight of my day and it was actually enjoyable a wasp coming into my room was actually like fun I think this is what people talk about when they say oh you know when you don't do it dopamine detox you have duck fried

dopamine receptors nothing really feels fun and then when you just cut out all of that basic kind of instant gratification fun activities suddenly everything just feels like it's fun again the smallest things I didn't really believe in the fried dopamine receptors

I don't know if there's science behind it but I'm guessing that bi fried dopamine receptors it kind of referred into like building up a tolerance of dopamine because you do build up tolerance to pretty much anything including you know all substances obviously drugs in junk food and then I'm assuming you probably do to just instant gratification activities because you build up a tolerance to Netflix to readinggames they just feel less fun the more you play them that's my opinion anyway and so when you quit and you have a tolerance break it just makes the effect of the substance just come back so I'm thinking that essentially when you do a dopamine detox it's kind of like just having a tolerance break from like smoking weed or from eating junk food or something where the effect of it just feels after you've had a few days off for a week off or however long off the effects of it just feel more that's the best way to put it just they feel like you have more effect from that substance or maybe even from any substance I was quite bored on the internet I feel like a lot of people could relate to that even with the internet even with everything that you've got on there you can be bored and that's so weird you've got access to virtually like anything on the internet and you do anything you watch movies you scroll on Reddit and you're still bored isn't that weird that we've got that much stuff and you're literally just bored because you've just done it too much it is really everything in moderation you and you need that balance and the problem is I actually commented this on someone's reddit post was that this kind of everything in moderation think it shouldn't be used as an excuse to say that oh playing your ps4 is okay because everyone who says it you know oh no playing readinggames in moderation is okay the reason why I disagree is because none of you [___] who play readinggames know what moderation is there isn't a single teenager male who's out there right now during lockdown who played in moderation if he's an active person who plays games like if he considers himself a gamer he's not gonna be playing in moderation he's gonna be playing like eight hours a day no one knows what moderation is anymore because we can't moderate our own addictions and our parents used to do that for us but now our parents are addicted as well I can I can guarantee that all of the kids who you know the kids and teenagers who are playing reading games at fortnight for like 10 hours a day their parents are also addicted to the Internet and that's why they're allowed to play for 10 hours a day that's kind of like a trap now they can't come out of it their parents aren't gonna help them to come out of it I don't think I can convince like a little teenager who's addicted to the Internet and [___] I don't think I can convince him to do a dopamine detox but I know someone who's already in this kind of community someone's were already browsing the subreddit someone who's already even tried their own dopamine detox it's like we've got so much more in common being you if you're still watching this reading15 minutes in that means that you don't have as fried dopamine receptors as you may think if you've sat and literally just watched me ramble that means that your attention span is actually decent and this is the era of social media people are used to scrolling down and within half a second seeing something new so a readingwhere you just set the camera there and talk it just people lose interest rate away because the first thing they'll do is scroll down to the comments you know just check and now I do that as well because you need that extra dopamine hit while the guy's just blabbing on and the second thing to do is check out the suggested videos and click on the next one because it's just another dopamine hit clicking on the next YouTube reading is like scrolling down on social media so now that we're like 10 15 minutes into this readinglike I said in my previous long one that pretty much means that all the people with short attention spans have already clicked off onto the suggested videos or whatever and the only people who are still gonna be watching this are obviously gonna be the ones who actually interested in this concept kind of it's obvious isn't it but it kind of when I realized that I was quite I was actually excited because that now gives me a moment to talk like unfiltered when I started like getting deep in my last long readingand so many people commented saying that and I feel like I actually helped people so first of all if we're 15 minutes in and I get to like talk just real I want to say like I'm literally grateful for you watching this right now I know you don't see this in like YouTube videos and like I'm literally addressing you like who's you right now like this is honestly my full-time job like that obviously I'm not getting paid for I'm not making any money from it but I quit my job I moved out of the city I moved back home with my parents to purposely be able to spend literally 6 to 10 hours a day on YouTube I've always wanted to be a youtuber but only because it's like the platform that completely understand and allows me to talk just like this and so that's what I've wanted to do like my entire life is teach these kind of concepts that can better your life I've been on this self-improvement grind since I was about 17 and a half 18 and it has changed my life so much there are downside like I've mentioned like you do lose some friends but you gain so much higher quality ones I've heard that guys who stop playing readinggames stop smoking we stop

hanging around with the same guys and I
start going to like exercising they start going
to the gym and joining clubs but their
original group of friends just turn hateful
towards them and maybe that's just us with
our big egos thinking that everyone hates us
and everyone's thinking about us honestly I
feel like a bit of like half of half of what we're
feeling is about our ego but the other half is
true people it scrubs in a book it mentality no
one wants to see someone else climb out I
shouldn't say no one low value people don't
want to see someone else climb out crabs
don't want to see another crab climb out of
the book here but a high value person is
already at th

Conclusion

Is a dopamine detox suitable for everyone?
While a dopamine detox can be beneficial for
many people, it may not be appropriate for
individuals with certain mental health
conditions or those who rely on specific

activities for therapeutic purposes. It's essential to consult with a healthcare professional before starting any detox regimen, especially if you have underlying health concerns.

To maintain the benefits of a dopamine detox, it's essential to adopt healthy habits and lifestyle changes that support balanced dopamine levels and overall well-being. This may include establishing boundaries around digital devices, practicing mindfulness, prioritizing self-care, and finding joy in simple pleasure.
es.